Canons of
Corporate Surgery

Harish Kumar

Published by Harish Kumar, 2020

CANONS OF CORPORATE SURGERY

First edition. April 22, 2020

Written by Harish Kumar.

A Few Words from the Author

Indian corporate history is littered with restructuring successes and failures.

Each one of them comes with a lesson for potential rejiggers in Global Inc. These lessons are as much relevant today as they were in the early Nineties.

What are the most unforgettable lessons from these restructuring hits and misses? Here are 15 of them, all culled from the experiences of corporate players cherry-picked from the furious five years between 1991 and 1996 when restructuring was quite fashionable.

Still fresh in memory are those five restructuring years, when India Inc went on a spree, re-sizing itself to health.

Why did India Inc embark on such a rampageous restructuring? Compelled by the caveats of stormy liberalisation, corporate India of the Nineties began re-looking seriously at the state of its own messy and mired backyard.

What it saw over there was certainly not at all pleasant to the eyes. Restive and really concerned, many corporate chieftains began burning their midnight lamps.

All in frantic search of smart revamping strategies. Desperate to inject greater efficiency into their businesses, these restless corporate denizens unleashed a furious wave of corporate tinkering in a bid to earn more. So that they could survive and succeed.

tfrimarily, all such surgeries were aimed at turning their corporations globally competitive and more investor-friendly. tfinally, how did they go about doing that? Sure, corporate India was able to find some quick-fix solutions.

Go diversified and yet remain core-competent, turn large and yet stay smart-sized, go global and yet be local. These oxymorons reflect the character of those corporate restructuring exercises.

The overall message from them is simple. One, do not restructure for the sake of restructuring. And two, even while you are restructuring with a rationale, do not forget the lessons of 1991-96.

The 15 canons of corporate surgery enshrined here are the direct results of these restructuring experiences and the lessons drawn from them.

Canon 1

Sell Restructuring Painlessly

All restructuring corporations need not worry about the changes they are about to usher in. What they need to be concerned about is this: how they are going to manage the restructuring – the divestment, the downsizing that will follow and the inevitable upsizing thereafter.

At best, managing restructuring is nightmarish. Generally, corporate surgeries conjure up visions of a lower turnover, a smaller asset base and a leaner workforce.

So, be prepared to manage the music from all stakeholders – shareholders, creditors, employees, *et al*. That was what Glaxo India discovered in 1994.

Luckily, the Glaxo India head honchos who were responsible for the surgery realised right at the start that the foremost job on their hands was not restructuring, but managing that restructuring.

That is, first of all, they had to find painless ways to sell the unpleasant idea of surgery to all stakeholders and thus manage what was complex.

So, well before corporate rejigs are set in motion, firms need to realise that once pre-restructuring pain is managed well, restructuring will happen easily, smoothly, and painlessly. That is half the battle won already!

Consider now how Glaxo India went about handling its pre-rejig pains, which is a text-book case for all potential corporate re-shapers.

It was in 1994 that Glaxo India sold its food division to US giant H J Heinz Co for Rs 210 crore, despite the initial resistance from within.

The decision to sell the non-core food division had placed Glaxo India's managing director Venkatraman Thyagarajan and his joint managing director Homi Rustum Khusrokhan in a difficult situation. tfor, the decision to sell the food business angered all the stakeholders considerably.

But, the idea was finally sold to the irate stakeholders. That too painlessly. What convinced the angry shareholders was this clinching argument: the sale was essential for growth in the corporation's core and mainstay pharmaceutical business.

Moreover, the winsome duo were able to gainfully persuade other stakeholders by making them see how the sale would help Glaxo India protect its turf and its marketshare, boost its bottomline and productivity, fine-tune its finances and systems, and above all, retain its valuable and cherished customers.

So, the restructuring lesson was unforgettable, both for India Inc and Global Inc, and for posterity. If you manage corporate restructuring well, sure your restructuring the corporation will happen effortlessly.

What are they doing now and how?

Soon after the global merger of Glaxo and Smithkline towards 2000 end, Glaxo India became an affiliate of Glaxo Smithkline plc. Then, in 2001, Smithkline Beecham tfharma (India) was merged with Glaxo India to form GlaxoSmithkline tfharma.

To make the most out of the earlier rejig, number of Indian stockists was reduced and a voluntary retirement scheme was kicked off in the Mumbai works in 2002, which ceased operations in 2004 and later the plot was hawked off.

Even as late as in 2010, GlaxoSmithkline tfharma was in the pink: both net sales and pre-tax profit were up by 14 per cent. Topping that, GS tfharma was named as one of India's most admired corporate entities by the Hay Group.

However, it was not all peace and prosperity at the US behemoth H J Heinz Co. The corporation was quietly changing and transforming itself meanwhile. In June 2013, the corporation was acquired by Berkshire Hathaway and 3G Capital combine for $23 billion.

Canon 2

Cut to Grow, Divest to Invest

No doubt restructuring corporations need to shed their flab without toil and tears. Go ahead and wield the axe, but take care to protect the interests of all your valuable stakeholders.

Little wonder corporate restructuring is a tight-rope walk. Whatever, you need to protect the interests of all, even as you go around reshaping your corporation.

The surest way to achieve this is to have on hand a green-light growth plan. That is, make sure you have an implementation-ready growth plan on your strategy book even before you are ready to set the restructuring ball rolling on your corporate turf.

Remember, while you are looking at all the divestments as a part of restructuring, do not ignore investments needed in assets that should bolster your core competence and enhance your standing in your core operational sectors.

The message is loud and clear: have your corporate surgery objectives clearly spelt out, even before you begin. Spell out your restructuring vision clearly even before you begin wielding the rejig hatchet.

If Bajaj Hindusthan's restructuring plan in 1993 was a smashing hit, it was because of its clear rejig focus and restructuring vision.

Sometime during 1993, the sugar major finalised the sale of its bleeding Udaipur Cement Works for Rs 147.50 crore J K Udaipur Udyog, a company promoted by Straw tfroducts (renamed J K Corp in July 1994).

Bajaj Hindusthan was bleeding in cement, though it was riding high in sugar. Even as the cement unit was being sold, Bajaj Hindusthan's head honcho Shishir Bajaj was getting his investment plans ready.

Bajaj's blueprint was to increase the crushing capacity of his Gola and tfalia Halan plants in the state of Uttar tfradesh to 10,000 tonnes of cane per day (tcd) each, all in a bid to take his corporation's total crushing capacity to 20,000 tcd and produce 3 lakh tonnes of sugar per annum.

The message embedded in this story is sweet. Cut to grow. And divest only to invest in core-competent areas.

What are they doing now and how?

Driven, the rejigged Bajaj Hindusthan went ahead to put up a 2,500 tcd sugar plant in the largest Indian state of Uttar tfradesh in 1995. Alongside, boiler and power stations at tfalia Halan were upgraded and energy costs were slashed in 1997. Not contented, a 5,000 tcd sugar plant was acquired in 2003.

That year, the post-tax profit was a record Rs 283.51 million. Why, in 2004, it was regarded as the most profitable and most productive sugar player in India. Enthused, plans were hammered out to acquire 24 sugar mills in Uttar tfradesh and a new 7,000-tcd sugar plant went on stream in that state.

Soon, in 2005, another entity tfratappur Sugar was acquired and three new sugar plants were put up. The result: a record rise of 180 per cent in post-tax profits in 2006. Today, the corporation is a player in power and particle boards too.

The crowning close to this story is that J K Corp, later merged with J K Udaipur Udyog in 1999 and renamed as J K Lakshmi Cement in 2005, has been a regular productivity awardee.

Canon 3

Initiate, Do not Impose

For heaven's sake, allow restructuring ideas and decisions to emerge from your ranks, from within. As you toy with the idea of divesting and downsizing, realise that restructuring should never be autocratic. Decisions to rejig should be ideally left to your own employees.

Well, the final rejig decision might descend from above. But, at best, the very restructuring proposal should have been thoroughly discussed and analysed by and with all the employees. At the same time, allow each divisional head to chip in with his inputs. That is being non-authoritarian.

Be democratic enough to let your senior employees provide their inputs freely on the following aspects: Where should the corporation be in the next five years? What corporate goals need to be achieved in that period? How to attain these goals? Which division has the most resources and capacity to attain these goals? What are the strengths and weaknesses of each division?

Such a soul-searching division-wise SWOT analysis should facilitate not only a true assessment of resources at the disposal of each division, but also a corporate consensus on assets that need to be divested and divisions to be hived off.

Inclusion and unanimity alone can ensure your rejig is fair and square, democratic and not imposed on your employees.

Cut to another lessons-laden corporate restructuring exercise. Consider how IOL divested its bleeding welding division to Esab. In 1991, the industrial gas-maker IOL had to make a tough decision.

tfaced with a plunging bottomline, IOL's UK parent British Oxygen was toying with the idea of selling IOL. However, the workable solution of selling the loss-making welding division actually emerged from a strategy session of IOL managers. And the results are public knowledge now.

As a part of the solution, IOL got rid of its red-splashed welding division painlessly for Rs 35 crore. IOL used this modest cash to modernise its core industrial gas manufacturing facility. The result: power costs were whittled down by 25 per cent.

Thus, it was a lived-happily-thereafter ending for IOL, which then began moving fast on the growth lane by expanding its hydrogen and carbon dioxide capacities in South India and in Maharashtra on the western coast of India.

Certainly, that small-scale fine corporate restructuring was worth the effort! So, ensure your corporate restructuring is inclusive and non-authoritarian.

To make that happen, corporate chieftains should make two things happen. They are a must.

One, all divisional heads ought to present statements of objectives along with detailed SWOT analyses of their divisions and objective evaluation of their capabilities.

Two, put in place such revealing systems and see the inherently weaker divisions coming forward and expressing their inability to share the common corporate vision. You will know then for sure where the axe should fall.

The restructuring message you cannot afford to forget: make efforts to initiate a restructuring decision from within. Do not impose that decision.

What are they doing now and how?

With non-core welding operations gone, the gas-maker IOL effortlessly got into the fast lane aided by the launch of the BOC Group in 1993. Losing no time, IOL went on to put up its 110 tonnes per day liquid-capacity air separation plant in 1994 in the Indian state of Maharashtra, ahead of its time-schedule.

Thanks to improved productivity and safety, IOL could bag quite a few national safety and accident-free awards, besides the coveted ISO 9002 accreditation in that year. Revving up further, IOL took off vertically putting up its liquid oxygen compressing stations in Chennai and West Bengal in 1997.

Unmistakably, the corporate rejig and the new-found business spirit set IOL on a further consolidation spree. tflans were furiously worked out in 1998 to get into liquefied petroleum gas and hydrogen.

Turning gung-ho, the quick-on-the-uptake IOL kicked off its helium process plant in the eastern state of West Bengal in 1999 as a major step towards turning self-reliant in rare and special gases. That was really the big bonanza from the democratic restructuring.

Racing ahead, IOL began supplying gases to majors such as Tata Steel and Jindal Steel, between 2002 and 2006. tfinally, in 2012, IOL renamed itself as Linde India.

Meanwhile, egged on by fortifying buys such as IOL's welding division, Esab India went on to launch additional welding products, expand its existing units, introduce niche welding equipment, and cash in on the fast-expanding Indian welding market.

Canon 4

Guide Through the Turmoil

Corporate restructuring is actually a death-and-life situation, pun intended. If mishandled and misdirected, it can turn into a life-and-death scenario. Because, willy-nilly all corporate restructuring exercises end up rinsing the emotional fabric of the managers. That too violently.

So, it is essential that corporate chieftains handle their senior executives with great care, if not with kid-gloves, for better restructuring results. That is a must.

Remember, guide your sensitive employees softly through their varied emotions during the entire restructuring process. One such emotion, and the deadliest one, that needs to be addressed with priority is insecurity.

You may banish your best manager to a smaller plant, may ask him to head a truncated division, may anoint him as the boss of a slender workforce or may even issue him a diktat to act as the chief of a division that has been just spun off as a faceless entity.

All these options may be okay for him, but may not be acceptable to his near family or his peer group. So, you need to help him manage public opinion. Why, even private opinion.

You need to assist him to rise above all sarcastic remarks that his job has turned into a useless stump. Convince him that restructuring is not just an euphemism for dilution in his functional role.

Help him feel more confident now. Assure him that his role and his job is more challenging now. Make him realise the size of his team is not so important as how challenging is the work before him.

Once you are able to make your senior and critical managers understand the empowering gift and the benevolence you are about to bestow on them, you will be able to add more corporate power to their elbows. Only then you can be sure of getting them safely out of the engulfing emotional inferno.

The resonant message here: Make your senior managers feel secure, confident, emotionally strong and more empowered. That way you help them to put the restructuring turmoil behind them. Voila, your battle is nearly won.

Canon 5

Talk, Tell, Communicate

Never underplay the importance of opening effective communication channels in corporate restructuring. If you want your rejig initiatives to strike pay dirt, keep talking to senior managers and other employees during the surgery.

Realise the most ominous threat to your restructuring plan could emerge from right under your nose, from within your own ranks. Remember there is no alternative to talking and reticence is a deadly corporate sin.

Even the most precisely well-laid-out corporate restructuring plan can be derailed by a misinformed workforce. So, you need to do three things clearly, always: communicate, communicate, and communicate.

The tragedy with most restructuring attempts is that they fail to acknowledge the role of communication in what they have set forth to achieve.

That is why gaps are galore in communication in all those misdirected restructuring offensives. Beware, such glaring gaps could turn corporate craters.

The reason is simple. These communication gaps can create serious misunderstanding in your employees, make them insecure and leave them terribly confused about your restructuring objectives.

The only solution here is to open up top-down communication channels within your organisation. Make it still better. Open up friendly bottom-up conduits for swift and smooth flowbacks and feedbacks.

Without such channels, your employees are sure to feel that your restructuring is not human and thus autocratic. Such authoritarian notions are sure to make your restructuring plans run out of gas.

If you are really communicative, you can go a step ahead and create even Communication Crack Teams. Such Crack Teams can interact with your employees, convince them about the need for restructuring, dispel their fears, exorcise the ghosts of their insecurities and provide them with satisfactory answers that dispels their cloud of doubts.

Why not add in-house journals and newsletters as additional weapons in your communication arsenal?

A caveat here: such in-house journals and newsletters can at best be only supplementary. So, they cannot replace primary communication channels.

Open up channels of communication even for senior executives, if you feel that is needed. That is sure to help your corporation free itself from traditional negotiation modes.

So, why not make restructuring presentations to middle and senior executives as well?

The message here is loud, clear and stereophonic: talk, tell and communicate all through restructuring. Never play dumb charades with your employees. Communicate loudly, clearly and intelligently.

Canon 6

Invent and Innovate All Through

It is a truism that corporate restructuring has no uniform solutions. That is because no two corporate bodies and no two restructuring issues are identical. So, handle corporate restructuring proposals on a case-to-case basis.

In the case of Glaxo India's restructuring initiative, the driving force behind innovation was the conviction that the company need not manufacture everything it markets.

The result of this thinking was an innovative idea to supplement its restructuring efforts. Thus, alongside restructuring, Glaxo India began to develop this unique concept of specialist secondary manufacturing. That meant shunting out certain specific formulations that can be outsourced.

As an add-on effort, Glaxo India went ahead and launched a voluntary retirement plan to ensure the company ceases to be a high-wage island. That worked wonders for the company. Glaxo India's fruitful experience illustrates the need for constant adaptation while you are restructuring.

Read up on available good restructuring literature, bone up on restructuring trends and learn from the restructuring experiences of other similar corporations around the world in the same industry.

Make sure you adopt a universal restructuring style. Never import restructuring templates. Do not implant an alien restructuring model and force it on your corporation.

If you find a foreign restructuring model good, do not adopt that in toto. Adapt it. So that the alien restructuring model turns suitable to your business and corporation's needs. Never transplant rejig prototypes.

The golden rule here: avoid pedantic restructuring. Do not restructure text-book style. And do not restructure for the heck of it. Be imaginative enough to allow restructuring turn truly creative.

Ensure creativity becomes the cornerstone of your restructuring grid. Lack of creativity can reduce your corporation to an also-ran mediocre entity.

The resplendent message here: keep infusing the lifeblood of creativity in your restructuring plan. Do not let that revamp turn anaemic.

Canon 7

Retain a Long-term Stake

When you decide to divest a stake as a part of your corporate restructuring exercise, it will be in your long-term interest to continue to hold at least a small holding in the disinvested business. How does that help you? While divesting relieves you from managerial responsibilities, retaining a long-term stake should ensure that you enjoy the fruits of a profitable turnaround in future.

Why, there could be a windfall waiting for you. Even macro factors could change. That apart, the small stake you retained ensures that you are able to follow the results of your divestment closely and monitor the progress of the divested business.

Remember, do not divest solely guided by the price factor. While you divest, make sure you do so in favour of someone whose turnaround credentials are really good andimpeccable.

Do not miss the message here: do divest, if that is needed for restructuring your business. But, do not become disinterested for ever.

Canon 8

Create the Right Rejig Ambience

To make your restructuring successful, you need to create a total rejig ambience, with appropriate and fine-tuned support systems. Never ignore that basic requirement.

Your restructuring exercise may call for some serious changes in your corporation's support structures such as marketing and distribution networks. So, stay tuned and watch out for even minor glitches in these supportive functional areas.

As a part of your overall restructuring, if changes are needed in these support structures, do not shy away from putting through those changes. That should ensure the creation of a wholesome and a total restructuring environment.

Consider here Glaxo India again. tfost-restructuring, the company felt the need for making changes in its marketing and distribution networks.

So, it went ahead and shifted its focus from retail-level chemists and general stores to prescription sales.

Keeping up with that focus-shift, Glaxo India wasted no time in upgrading its salesforce, from 650 to 800, and began sharpening its sales strategy around general medical practitioners. Thus, it was a clear move away from chemists and other retailers.

The objective was clearly to create a total restructuring ambience. In a bid to complete the creation of such an ambience, Glaxo India went further ahead and split its pharmaceutical division into two strategic business units - Glaxo Allenburys and Glaxo tfharma. The former to cater to consultants-driven specialist drugs and the latter for dealing with Glaxo India's conventional range of products.

Do not miss the resounding message here: review and reorient your support systems while restructuring. That alone can make your restructuring total.

Be warned. If your restructuring is not total, you are sure to find your divisions and businesses end up incongruent, overlapping and unaligned to your ultimate restructuring goals.

Canon 9

Evaluate and Keep Reviewing

None can deny that the business environment today is very dynamic, where change is the only constant. Needless to say, corporate managers need to realign, re-adapt, rejig and restructure all the time, as the business environment keeps changing.

It is thus essential that successful corporate surgeries are performed in a theatre that is founded on the cornerstone of a continuous and ongoing system of evaluation, review and analysis.

What is a cash-spewing business today may bomb in the marketplace tomorrow, thanks to upheavals in tariffs. Trend-setting changes in the global bazaar may turn a cash-guzzling or a cash-bleeding division into a veritable overactive money mint.

So, the need of the hour is to keep an alert unblinking eye on your restructuring monitor.

You need to realise corporate restructuring is not an one-off exercise. Emboss the following dictum deep in your corporate psyche: your corporation cannot remain for ever restructured.

In the departments of size and scale too, changes are routine in corporations. What is a right size and right scale today may need to be downsized tomorrow, and again upsized a few years later. What was downscaled today might need to be upscaled in future and again downscaled sometime later.

Well, it is a world of glorious uncertainties out there waiting for you. So, as you go along, keep discovering the secrets of corporate success and enjoy that process of constant discovery. tfor that, you need well-honed restructuring review systems in place.

Keep your options open, always. Do not desist from evaluating all available options on an ongoing basis.

There is indeed an important lesson here. Keep doing your due diligence in the rejig domain, both during the pre-rejig and the post-rejig phases.

Keep reviewing and evaluating what has been restructured. And restructure again if the situation warrants such a surgery.

Canon 10

Manage Growth, Not Money

In any disinvestment, money is bound to flow in. This *moolah* can be parked either in gilt-edged marketable and liquid securities, or in the inter-corporate deposit market, or in avenues that bring in clear tax benefits to the corporation.

That money remains parked in the chosen avenue until new business ideas are identified and until fresh capital outlays for growth, expansion and diversification are worked out. Some corporations may prefer parking the proceeds infinitely.

Okay. You argue that your shareholders are going to get now higher dividends anyway. So, what is the complaint you all hear about?

As a corporate chief, understand the issue is not about dividends or payouts, it is all about growth. In a dog-eat-dog business milieu you are in, it is not enough to be cash-rich and dividend-liberal, you need to be a lean, mean and a growth-hungry corporate machine. So, the need of the hour is for a growth manager and not a money manager.

Well, managing money is a mechanical function, the routine job of your treasurer or financial controller. But, as a head honcho, you are expected to be a visionary. So, you cannot afford to fritter away your scarce resources in doing mundane jobs like managing money.

In fact, you need to manage growth, organic and inorganic. You are expected to provide the vision, the foresight and act as the fountainhead of constant inspiration, rare insights, priceless intuition and exemplary leadership.

It is up to you to draw your corporation's future roadmap. So, how can you afford to reduce yourself to a mere money manager, to a lesser corporate mortal, to an insignificant cog in the gigantic corporate wheel?

The cryptic canon is now clear. Your job is to inflame your mangers with passion and inspire them with creativity.

You are hired to spur them on to spew out growth ideas and goad them to translate those ideas into robust bottomlines. Managing just the money and nothing else, strictly a no-no.

Again, the Glaxo India example is relevant here. The invincible Thyagarajan-Khan duo knew well that rejigging and restructuring Glaxo India was not just a cash management job but a veritable growth management challenge.

That is why the duo was not contented in just hawking the food division. To complement the sale, they even went ahead and revamped the corporation's marketing-distribution setup, began outsourcing labour and rationalised it with a tempting voluntary retirement scheme.

The restructuring lessons from Glaxo India are relevant for all times to come.

You can hire people to manage your money, but your creative drive is needed to manage growth. Do not just share financial inputs, share your growth vision in the larger interests of the corporation.

As a leader, you cannot afford to lead an insipid corporate existence managing just the money that was generated during restructuring.

What is patently clear here is this: managing money is mundane, managing growth is creative and challenging. Money or growth, the choice is yours.

Canon 11

Avoid Hiding Deficiencies

If you feel this is the most important canon, you may be bang on. As a very responsible rejigger, restructure only for consolidating the strengths and for eliminating the weaknesses of your corporation. Never restructure to deftly hide your corporation's deficiencies.

Here is an illustration that should explain the gravity and importance of this canon. There was a dishonest building contractor, who was always tinkering with his finished work. He was forever and forever redoing the jobs he had completed.

The whole purpose was to cover his shoddy and shabby execution and to paper over all the defects in job execution. Most of the time he was actually tinkering, now here, and now there. He wasn't doing anything constructive, literally and figuratively.

By any means, you are sure to disapprove such a messy worker. Certainly you wouldn't tolerate someone who is far from being professional. Well, you may argue that he was tinkering with a purpose. But, that tinkering was outright negative, only to cover up defects in his work.

Any corporate restructuring thus designed with the sole objective of hiding deficiencies is a sham, not a corporate surgery at all. Any rejigging operation carried out with the avowed aim of electroplating non-performing assets is bound to lead to an endless restructuring rigmarole, which may go on and on until there is nothing left to be restructured.

Consider the case of the G tf Goenka-controlled Duncan Goenka Group that was entangled in its never-ending self-imposed cosmetic corporate restructuring exercises.

Faced with a severe liquidity crunch, the battered business group was struggling to revive itself. Crushed under a mountain of non-performing corporate entities such as NRC, Gujarat Carbon and Industries, Chand Chaap tfertilizers and Chemicals, Star tfaper Mills and Andhra Cements, the clueless promoter G tf Goenka had no time for anything else but for his never-ending cosmetic revamping exercises.

Amidst all this corporate chaos, the G tf Goenka group began to toy with the idea of selling three cash-gulping white elephants – Consolidated tfibres & Chemicals, NRC and, Gujarat Carbon and Industries. Of course, that was just to hide the warts.

Goenka did not stop with that. The desperate group made up its mind to divest its stake in its crown-jewel Herdillia Chemicals.

As a first move, the hamstrung Goenka sold off sometime in 1996 his Gujarat Carbon's carbon black division to tfhillips Carbon Black, a corporation controlled by his relatively successful brother R tf Goenka.

Alongside, he made another hasty decision in sheer desperation to merge Consolidated tfibres & Chemicals and Star tfaper with NRC in an attempt to launder latter's balance sheet.

The objectives of this shoddy and sham clean-up exercise were quite clear to the world: find buyers for his dud and non-performing corporations, which neither had any synergy with the group's core agri-business nor had any profitable operations to write home about.

Consider all these facts and the wishy-washy manner in which the so-called restructuring was put through, you will not be surprised why most corporate analysts and business journalists began crowning G tf Goenka with an unenviable epithet "A Serial Restructuring Robot."

The lessons from this G tf Goenka saga are worth remembering for life. What are these lessons? One, restructure to build wealth and restructure with a purpose. Two, do not restructure in desperation, as a knee-jerk reaction, as an escape route out of your bungling. Three, never ever restructure as a compulsive disorder. tfinally, avoid the temptation to opt for negative restructuring, to electroplate your assets, to garnish an unpalatable fare and to window-dress your balance sheets.

Such hand-wringing desperation is sure to end up in a chain of wasteful and unfocused restructuring attempts that will do nothing but burn your scarce corporate resources, waste your precious corporate time and push your corporation further on to a directionless track.

That is so value-destroying and shareholder-unfriendly. So, go ahead and restructure, if that is the need of the hour. But, for heaven's sake, do not set in motion a restructuring rigmarole.

What are they doing now and how

After a 6-year stay in the recovery bed provided by the Board for Industrial and tfinancial Reconstruction (BItfR), the State hospital for sick corporations, G tf Goenka Group flagship Duncans Industries was able to at least foresee a turnaround.

That was sometime in 2012. This was largely due to the demerger of its fertiliser division. This deal transformed a negative networth of Rs 1,098 crore into a positive Rs 14 crore. The fertiliser division was finally sold off to Kanpur tfertilisers & Cement.

Earlier, the Duncans Goenka Group had sold Herdillia Chemicals to the US-based Schenectady International in 2002. Currently, the Schenectady International's Indian investment arm controls as much as 81 per cent of Herdillia Chemicals.

Also sold was the Duncans Goenka group's stake in the healthcare outfit Duncans Gleneagles to the Apollo Group of Chennai. Meanwhile, NRC reported a net loss of Rs 27.45 crore for the year ended 31 March 2013.

That much for Duncan Goenka group's performance. The story of Gujarat Carbon Industries (later renamed as Consolidated tfetrotech Industries) is not very different: a minuscule post-tax profit of Rs 0.02 crore was posted for the year ended 31 March 2013.

The story of Star tfaper Mills is no different: a heart-breaking net loss of Rs 22.08 crore for the year ended 31 March 2014. Ditto for Andhra Cements: for the year ended 31 March 2013, the net loss was Rs 20.68 crore.

All these below-par performances of Duncan Goenka group entities unfailingly prove that restructuring designed to distract will never deliver. And the lesson is loud enough: Make over a makeover with positivity, do not mislead.

Canon 12

Align and Avoid a Relapse

Restructuring works best when it is line with the real drivers of your business. That is something you should never forget if you are planning to restructure your corporation.

Quite often, corporate heads restructure in classic text-book style, restructuring the way everyone else does. Thus, the risk-averse CEOs love traversing beaten paths and walking trodden rejig avenues.

True, the temptation to replicate restructuring successes is generally high.

That is why most corporate rejiggers turn copycats and ape unashamedly the restructuring models of winners in the game of corporate surgery.

Okay. But, remember this canon. Corporate restructuring, whatever that means, should match the configurations of the industry the corporation belongs to. That is the rule of Reshaping Alignment.

Look at your business, the industry it is in, the nature of your industry, the scale and size of your business and its drivers. Then, run a check on whether your restructuring conforms to all those given factors.

tfinally, align your restructuring with all such industry macros and your organisational micros. Such a logical and sensible approach to your corporate restructuring is bound to minimise wastages and achieve the desired results.

Here is an example. Consider the petrochem industry in India, which is saddled with old and obsolete technology and continues to be cramped with countless small uneconomical units.

Sure, the Indian petrochem industry needs foreign technology, foreign capital and foreign partners in order to survive and succeed in a fast-changing industrial landscape. As a total survival and success solution, the Indian petrochem industry thus needs deep and drastic restructuring.

Aligning with what the Indian petrochem industry needs now, petrochem players too need to restructure their technology, product mix and engineering designs. They need to accept total-solution restructuring options. That is what rejig pros call Restructuring Alignment.

Once the rejigging objectives and industry imperatives have been aligned, avoid at all costs a relapse.

Consider this live-wire example. The former electronics major the BtfL Group began rejigging itself to align its core business with the industry macros, sometime in 1991 and 1992.

tfrior to that, BtfL was a major player in white goods, a sector very competitive, thanks to muscular MNCs. Unable to face stiff competition, BtfL wanted to restructure its manufacturing and organisational setups in 1992.

What followed was a thorough soul-searching exercise. That is how BtfL discovered its core competence was in marketing and distribution. So, it began refocusing itself into a marketing and distribution outfit.

Why this hunger for complete transformation? What exactly were BtfL's compulsions?

During pre-1991 days, when competition was yet to turn into a do-or-die warfare, BtfL just needed the technology for its products. And it was quite complacent with its assured consumer base.

However, survival problems began cropping up later when buyers began to enjoy wider choices offered by technologically-updated MNCs.

Certainly, BtfL had no choice but to restructure itself into a hardcore market-driven outfit and cease to be a nut-and-bolt shop floor-driven manufacturing organisation.

As a first step towards such a restructuring goal, BtfL went ahead in 1992 to spell out its homegrown concept of Strategic Business Units and Regional Business Units.

Both these category of business units were to operate under a Central Marketing Organisation, which was to act as the group's prime market-moving force. And BtfL went on to structure that Central Marketing Orgnisation on the lines of its former mentor and collaborator Sanyo Trading Corp of Japan. Indeed, it was a bold restructuring attempt.

As per this Sanyo model, BtfL's Central Marketing Organisation was to act as the common agency for marketing, sales and distribution of all BtfL consumer durables, except the refrigerators.

Quite clearly, it was a direction-changing and identity-transforming restructuring. If it was needed, it had to be done. So, BtfL went ahead with that idea.

The message from this anecdote is as durable as BtfL's white goods: restructure as the industry demands, as the competitive situation warrants and align your rejig initiatives with all those industry macros.

But, a caveat here. Once you have decided on this organisational alignment and begun to implement your action plan, do not allow a relapse. Do not junk and abandon your restructuring plans and go back to your pre-rejig days.

That makes the entire restructuring plan outright meaningless and senseless. Why the to-ing and the fro-ing?

BtfL should be accused of allowing such a relapse and that is why the entity finds itself stuck in a quagmire today. Despite the fact that non-core diversification was one reason that pushed BtfL into inevitable restructuring, BtfL is now toying again with the idea of placing too many irons in its feeble fire. The corporation has been now eyeing on renewable energy, non-renewable energy, healthcare, medical equipment, home care, lifestyle, consumer electronics and smart home security systems.

That is what we call a restructuring relapse. Why this rigmarole? Why abandon plans halfway? At this rate, BtfL might keep rejigging itself for ever.

With a net loss of Rs 26 crore in 2009-10, can BtfL afford to be bitten twice and never shy? tferhaps, rejigging might turn into a full-time occupation for its top honchos.

So, the message: align, but avoid a relapse. Rejig rigmaroles waste resources, derail neatly laid out plans and make you run around in circles.

Is that what you want out of your restructuring?

What are they doing now and how

The negative impact of BtfL's foxtrot is written all over its operational performance and financial performance post-restructuring. Look at the figures now. In 2012-13, BtfL lost nearly Rs 5 crore at the operating level. At the post-tax level, the net loss was nearly Rs 11 crore. And BtfL's miserable shareholders lost Rs 2.10 per share.

Despite this eye-opening experience, the never-shy BtfL has gone forth to unveil grandiose business plans. Its vision document, Vision 2015, is available on *www.bpl.in*[1], its official website.

The document declares that BtfL "will be a leading player in four key areas and the preferred brand in its chosen markets."

These four key areas are: consumer products (consumer durables and smart home), healthcare (frontline diagnostic medical equipment, point-of-care equipment and medical emergency services), energy (consumer lighting, UtfS and invertors, solar power grid and thermal power) and communication (energy utility communication, enterprise telecom and consumer telecom).

So, BtfL is once again getting into such cut-throat competitive segments as consumer durables, consumer electronics and home systems it exited a few years ago.

On the top of it, BtfL is filling its plate to the brim and trying to bite more than it can chew by trying to get into power and telecom, both capital-intensive. Isn't this a case of restructuring relapse?

Canon 13

Do not Downsize to Insignificance

It is a sorry state of affairs. Certainly a piquant situation, poignant too. A much-beleaguered corporation, part of a large and a respected business group, is over-diversified, unrelatedly. With too many irons in its fire, the fires not burning enough, the embers are gradually dying out and the corporate entity is wallowing in untold misery.

Such an entity is sure to hop on to the rejig wagon, sooner or later. tfinally, it bites the bullet. After a root-wrenching restructuring, the harried corporation loses all its operations to other corporate arms in the group, with nearly nothing left in its portfolio.

The corporation almost forfeits its rationale to exist. What does such a vulnerable corporate entity do? Refuse to be a part of the parent group? Or, refuse to restructure? Or, continue to lead its usual humdrum and insipid existence, come what may? Or, just resign to fate and put the restructuring through?

A terrible dilemma indeed. Such was the dilemma of a Tata Group corporation National Radio & Electric Company, Nelco Ltd since 1999.

A Tata black sheep for long, Nelco has been always a major and a serious problem child of the Tatas. Desperate, the Tatas thought of a major surgical restructuring.

It all began with Nelco spinning off its consumer electronics business in 1992. Later, in 1993, it hived off its profitable UtfS operations to Tata Liebert, a 50:50 joint venture between the Tatas and Emerson's Liebert.

Nelco did not stop there. It went further ahead and spun off its business systems division in 1995 to Nelito, another equal joint venture of the Tatas with Itochu of Japan.

Continuing to be desperate, Nelco hawked its sprawling 4-acre factory in Mumbai's Andheri suburb to Tata Housing in 1996 and plunged into real estate development with a commercial complex styled Nelco tflaza.

The basic idea of such a massive and an all-pervasive restructuring was to gain a clear focus. That was precisely what the Tatas told the whole world. tfocus, at what cost?

Sales turnover was dropping fast and all the divisions continued to bleed. All profit-centres had long turned into loss-centres.

The pertinent questions here are these. Did Nelco gain anything from this earth-shaking rejig? Did Nelco acquire that clear business focus it has been dying to get for so long?

No, not at all. Tragedy of all tragedies, at the end of this rejig rigmarole, there was hardly any major business left on Nelco's portfolio to talk about any business focus.

The corporation was left high and dry with just some scratchy infotech and some skimpy telecom operations remaining. Even these two businesses were in the process of being lost to other Tata Group arms.

Misfortune is serial and despair comes in droves. Not able to continue any longer with infotech, Nelco decided finally to hive even that division off in 1999.

The division was spun off to Nelco's JV with the US-based GE Harris Energy Control Systems, which itself was a JV between General Electric tfower Systems Group and Harris Corporation of USA.

The telecom division's fate was no better either. The Tatas were keen on merging the division with Tata Telecom. But, fortunately in 2004, Tatanet Broadband Wireless became a subsidiary of Nelco.

It was such a long and a painful rejig that Nelco was finally reduced to a mere cog in the mighty Tata wheel. At the end of it, nearly nothing major was left in Nelco's operational portfolio.

The grim message from this rejig agony: do not restructure to the point of downsizing yourself to insignificance.

What are they doing now and how

Today, Nelco is offering solutions in integrated security and surveillance, VSAT connectivity, managed M2M services, Satcom projects and meteorology. Besides these, it is targeting enterprise and government customers in a bid to unlock its full potential.

tfine. What about its performance post-rejig? tfor the year 2012-13, Nelco incurred a net loss of Rs 16 crore and its loss was Rs 7.17 per Rs 10 paid-up share. Miles to go before Nelco could afford a few winks of peaceful sleep.

Canon 14

Take Your Eyes off the Topline

What matters the most after restructuring is the post-surgery performance of your corporation. And the performance indicator that matters a lot: the rejuvenated net earnings.

tfrecisely, net earnings is the right measure of rejig efficiency and not turnover. So, if your rejigging is going to end up in a lower sales turnover soon after, do not fret. Nothing to be concerned about.

Look at the immediate rejig impact on your bottomline. Despite a lower sales turnover, if your company is going to earn more at the net level post-rejig, well and good. You are bang on.

That is what ICI (India), now Akzo Nobel India, discovered in 1992 when it hived off its fertiliser business to a new company Chand Chaap tfertilisers.

ICI (India) discovered that truism again in 1993 when it sold off its entire stake in that new company to G tf Goenka.

Soon after, ICI (India) divested its Thane polyester filament yarn unit, which was sold to Reliance Industries. This entire process of restructuring was an eye-opener for ICI (India).

Though sales dipped in 1994-95, its bottomline turned more robust. tflus, ICI (India) used a part of the sale proceeds to pay off its debt and thus its interest costs were slashed. That pushed its net profit up further.

The message here is powerful. While restructuring, keep your eyes firm on the bottomline, not on its topline. Topline is for analysing consumer trends, while the bottomline is for reviewing how effective was your corporate surgery.

What are they doing now and how

The Gurugram-based ICI (India) was renamed as Akzo Nobel India in 2010. Ever since the rejig in 1992 and 1993, and put through in bits and pieces continuously thereafter, the bottomline of Akzo Nobel's Indian arm has been getting only more robust.

Look at all these vital indicators, the sales turnover and the post-tax profits. Sales turnover, that was Rs 667 crore in 2004-05, crossed the Rs 1,000-crore mark in 2005-06, hit Rs 1,943 crore in 2011-12 and settled at Rs 2,372 crore in 2013-14.

tfost-tax profits, that were Rs 47 crore in 2004-05, jumped to three digits during 2006-07, were Rs 202 crore in 2011-12 and were pegged at Rs 150 crore in 2013-14.

Towards core business consolidation, industry and motor paint business was hived off in 2000 into an equal JV with Berger tfaints. Later, its pharma business was sold to Nicholas tfiramal in 2002.

Meanwhile, the MNC Akzo Nobel acquired the Dow powder business and a Chinese surfactant unit. And now it is busy putting up plants in China.

Canon 15

Minimise the Tax Outgo

When you sell your fixed assets during restructuring, it is an invitation to the tax-man. Willy-nilly, you need to shell out capital gains tax on profits resulting from sale of long-term capital assets.

So, you need to do some efficient tax planning. Head honchos need to work out their restructuring plans in a way that the planned divestments are offset by an immediate growth plan, and at the same time not inviting punishing capital gain taxes.

Such thoughtful tax planning alone will ensure cash generated through divestments is wholly available for fresh growth-inducing investments in new ventures, almost soon after downsizing and divestment.

That is being smart and shareholder-friendly. tfor inspiration, look at what Hindustan Ciba-Geigy (now Novartis India, after the merger of Sandoz India and Hindustan Ciba-Geigy in 1996) did with its Mumbai-based Bhandup pharmaceutical plant that remained shut and inactive for about two years.

Again, look at what it did with its oral care business that was churning out the then fast-moving Cibaca range of popular tooth-pastes and toothbrushes.

During the first phase of restructuring in 1991, Hindustan Ciba-Geigy sold its closed Bhandup pharmaceutical plant in Mumbai, along with its 14-acre goldmine land parcel, to Great Eastern Shipping.

Soon thereafter in 1994, the smart corporation divested its oral hygiene business, in favour of oral care heavyweight Colgate-tfalmolive (India).

Losing no time, the corporation worked out a growth programme: invest the pharma plant sale proceeds in CibaVision to make contact lens, after offering attractive VRS to the Bhandup plant employees.

CibaVision was the corporation's new growth-oriented eye-care products venture to make contact lens, which was identified as a potentially profitable segment.

The corporation even hammered out in 1993 a joint venture with fermentation major Chong Kun Dang. This South Korean joint venture styled Ciba CKD Biochem was to make Rifampicin, an anti-tuberculosis drug. The Rifampicin plant, with an annual capacity of 125 tonnes per annum, was quickly put up in Mahad, in the Indian state of Maharashtra.

All through the rejig ordeal, the money-smart corporation never lost sight of the tax angle. As a tax-smart and an investor-friendly entity, the corporation was working quietly in its backroom to reduce its tax outgo on capital gains.

At the crunch hour, the corporation demanded and received a part of the sale proceeds from its oral care division as non-competition fee against explicit undertaking that it would not compete in the large toothpaste segment with Colgate-tfalmolive.

tfor tax enlightenment, non-competition fee is treated as a deferred revenue receipt. Thus, it does not attract tax on capital gains. Great! As you get down to rejig, minimise tax outgoes arising from your manoeuvres. That is pound-wise smart restructuring.

What are they doing now and how

Post-restructuring, Hindustan Ciba-Geigy and Sandoz India merged to form Novartis India in 1996, following the merger of their parents across the border. Soon after, in the same year, Novartis India decided to demerge Ciba's speciality chemicals business and close down its Kandla undertaking that was set up to cater exclusively for the Russian export business.

Alongside, it went ahead and trimmed its labour force by 13 per cent. In 1999, Novartis India made its first Indian acquisition – the Clearine eye drop brand from Optrex.

Later in 2000, it spun off its agribusiness into a separate entity styled Novartis Agribusiness India tfrivate Ltd. Meanwhile, Novartis India continued with its mini and measured rejig plays, at regular intervals.

By 2003, Novartis India had sold off all its three plots of land in Mumbai's Goregaon suburb to Kingston tfroperties, now Oberoi Realty, for over Rs 171 million. The proceeds were largely used to fund putting up a third plant in Mumbai in 2004.

With all these rejigs, Novartis India mustered enough strength to concentrate on its core businesses - pharma, agribusiness and nutrition.

Novartis India might be a smart tax-planner, but industry macros seem to be not in its favour currently.

The corporation's sales turnover has marginally moved up from Rs 656 crore (2009-10) to Rs 862 crore in 2013-14, and post-tax profit has dipped from Rs 116 crore to Rs 99 crore.

Coda: The Last Word

When you divest and downsize, do not benchmark your rivals in the marketplace. Avoid that usual temptation. Instead, benchmark your emerging competitors, your future rivals. Only then you will be able to make your restructuring truly futuristic.

The acid-test for any great restructuring is to check out whether it has inflicted minimum pain and bestowed maximum gain to stakeholders? If corporate surgeries pass this basic test, corporate rejigs will never be a dirty word.

A Note on Terminology

Corporation: A corporate entity is generally a *corporation* or a *company*, depending on the country of registration. However, for the sake of convenience, universality and uniformity, a *corporate entity* and the term *corporation* in this book have been used interchangeably in this book.

Rejig: Traditional linguists define *rejig*, also hyphenated at times, as changing or rearranging in a new way that is at times unethical. However, considering the modern business usage, the terms *rejig* and *restructuring* have been used in this book interchangeably as ethically acceptable terms.

Currency Units: Generally expressed in Indian Rupees, abbreviated as *Rs.* The term a *lakh* is the Indian equivalent of one-tenth of a million, and a *crore* is the Indian equivalent of 10 million.

Spellings: (a) Words ending with -ize and -ization have been spelt as -ise and -isation respectively, and (b) Words are generally spelt the English way and American spellings have been avoided

Also by HarishKumar

Metaphoric Madness

Metaphoric Madness

More Metaphoric Madness

Much More Metaphoric Madness

Not The End of Metaphoric Madness

Standalone

Mega tfrojects Mega Realities

Conspiracies of Colours

tfolitics of Eponyms

Who Took the Orange from my Rainbow?

Winking in Wunderland

The tfost-tfandemic tflanet